IF YOU KNOW,
YOU KNOW!
with Jamal

Hoda Elshayeb, Wala'a Farahat
& Buraidah Razack

Illustrated by Shireen Ahmed

If You Know, You Know with Jamal

Copyright @ 2023
Hoda Elshayeb, Wala'a Farahat & Buraidah Razack

Illustrated by Shireen Ahmed

YGTMedia Co. Press Trade Paperback Edition

Published in Canada, for Global Distribution by YGTMedia Co.

www.ygtmedia.co/publishing

ISBN 978-1-998754-21-2

Printed in North America

IF YOU KNOW, YOU KNOW!

with Jamal

Hey there! I'm Jamal. To be honest, I didn't expect to be on the cover of this book! I'm assuming it's because of my good looks since I usually don't get much attention. #middlechildsyndrome . . . ya know what I mean? Thanks, Mom and Dad! Low key, though, I've come to realize that center stage is overrated, *at least for me*. Now if I could only go back in time and tell this to thinks-he-knows-it-all, how-much-do-you-lift-bro, blinded-by-love-but-always-left-heartbroken Jamal. Bruh, if you could hear the stories of that Jamal as he went through puberty. Oh wait, I guess you can, and I guess you will! And that's right, I did say Puberty. Listen, it's really not what people make it out to be, and it's a lot less confusing when you don't have to figure it out all on your own.

Let's get into it,
and you can thank me later.

General Puberty

As a guy, I was hyper-focused on all the physical changes that came along with puberty and wanting to be a man. I was always wondering how everyone else managed, and if I was the only one that hadn't figured it out yet. Breaking news: you're not alone, and no one has it all figured out. Even if someone seems like they do, trust me, the struggle is real.

Puberty: A stage in your life when your body is going through many changes, both on the inside and outside, to get you ready to be an adult one day.

Puberty

Some of these changes take time, and it looks different for each person. If it takes longer, it doesn't necessarily mean something is wrong.

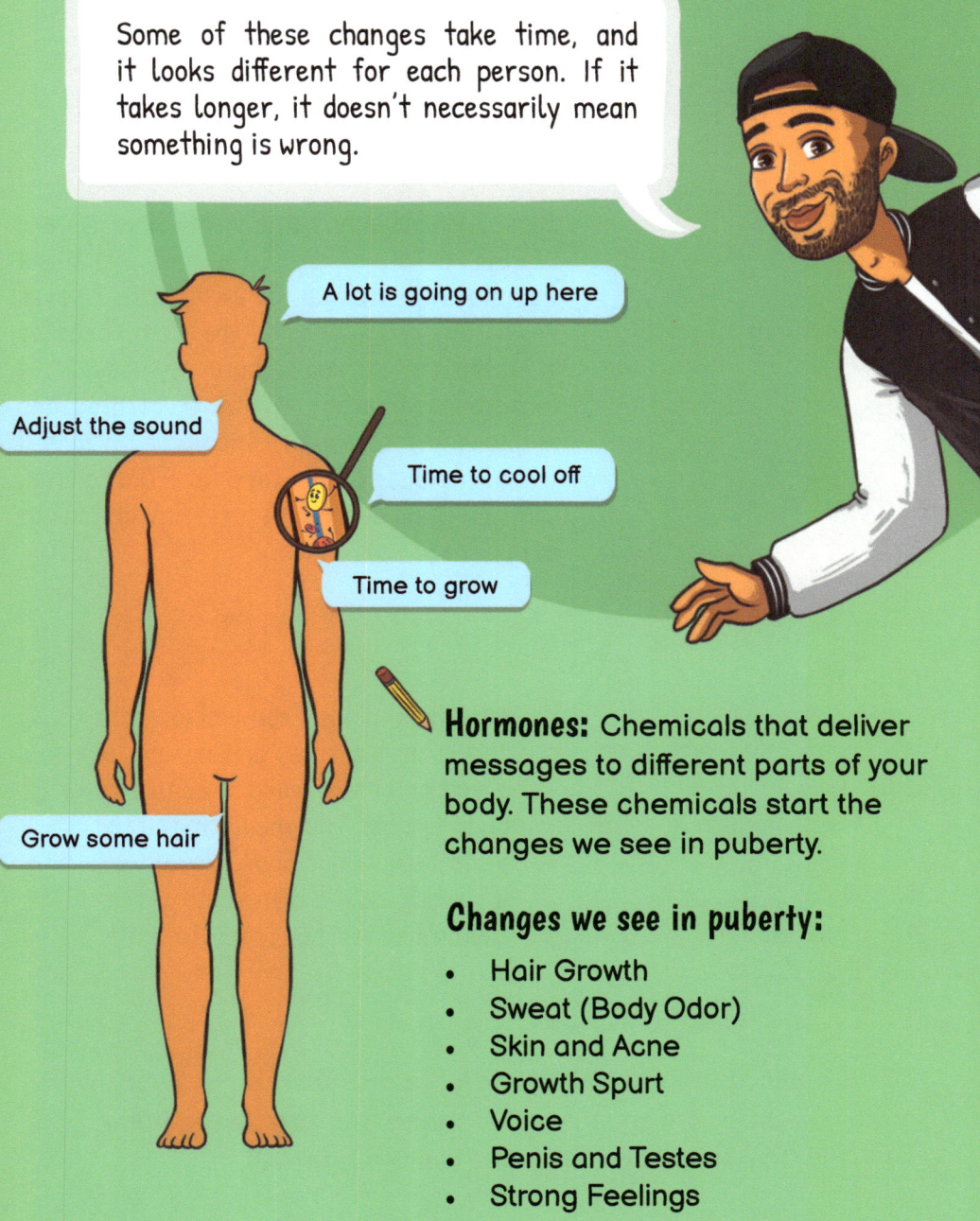

A lot is going on up here

Adjust the sound

Time to cool off

Time to grow

Grow some hair

Hormones: Chemicals that deliver messages to different parts of your body. These chemicals start the changes we see in puberty.

Changes we see in puberty:

- Hair Growth
- Sweat (Body Odor)
- Skin and Acne
- Growth Spurt
- Voice
- Penis and Testes
- Strong Feelings

These changes usually start with changes in your pubic area and hair growth. The truth is, when this happens, it doesn't mean you're an adult. Actually, you're not expected to act like one! Just continue being you and do the things you enjoy.

Growth Spurt

After I hit puberty, some of my friends were DEEZED at my age, and I always felt like I was playing catch up. To be honest, I never really enjoyed going to the gym, because even though I worked so hard, my body didn't look much different. I felt frustrated and helpless. In hindsight, the expectations I had of my body at the time were unrealistic. But now it's a different story. I mean look at me . . . need I say more?

All jokes aside, remember that this is not a race, and no one is ahead or behind when it comes to body image. The media may lead us to believe our body should look a specific way, but in reality, that couldn't be further from the truth.

Before hitting puberty, lifting weights and working out can help you tone your muscles and make them stronger, but it won't build new muscle or make them bigger yet.

See this right here could've saved me a lot of blood, sweat, and tears.

Most boys go through a growth spurt between the ages of 10 and 16. Sometimes this includes changes in height, broadening shoulders, feet, hands, arms, legs, and more muscle. If your legs and feet grow faster than the rest of your body, you may feel a little off-balance or clumsy. This will go away as your body continues to grow.

When your body is quickly changing and growing you may also feel achy, particularly in your thighs, knees, and calves. This is normal; heating pads, stretching, and massaging the area can help.

Many boys also notice some swelling in the chest area. This is caused by changes in hormone levels and is temporary.

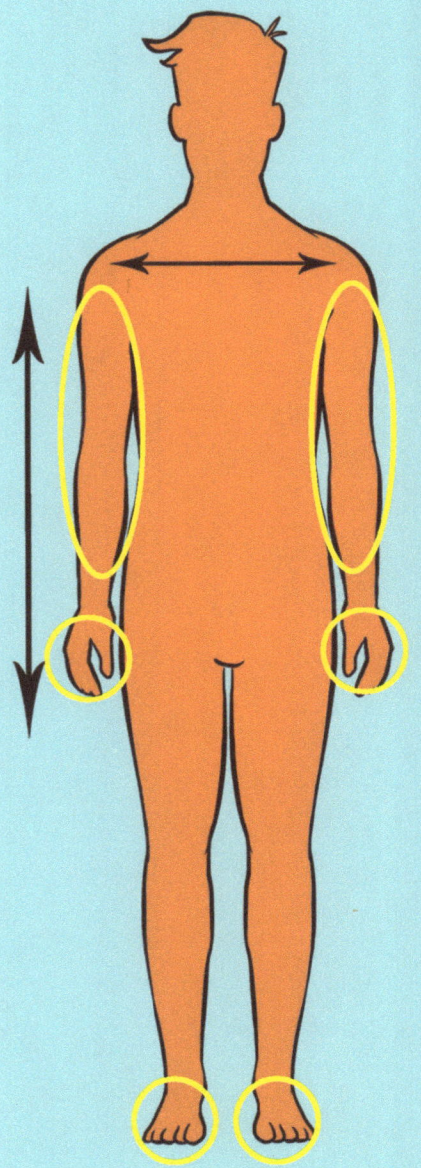

 Check out the "In a Pickle" section at the end for swelling chest area

Voice

BEFORE

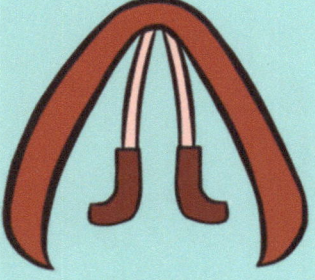

AFTER

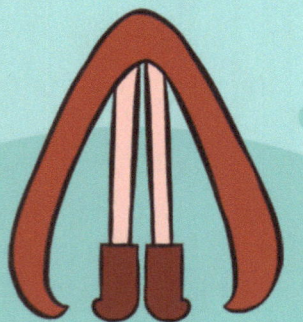

Boys usually notice changes in their voice between the ages of 11 and 14, and sometimes it occurs earlier or later.

What causes the change in your voice? Your larynx gets bigger, and your vocal cords grow longer and thicker. Your face structure actually changes too. Facial bones grow, so do the sinuses, nose, and throat. This creates more space for sounds to echo, which results in the change in your voice.

Why do guys' voices crack sometimes? It's because they're adjusting to all these changes. This can take a couple of months.

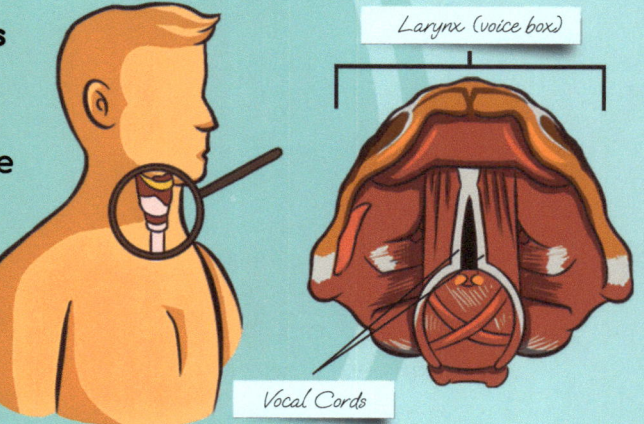

Larynx (voice box)

Vocal Cords

When your larynx gets bigger, it tilts in your neck. When it tilts, a part of it sticks out at the front of the throat. For some people, you can see a small bulge there called the Adam's apple, and for others, it isn't visible.

Sure, I have the voice of an angel now, but it wasn't always like this. One day my voice just sounded different, and it would randomly become high pitched. It totally threw me off, especially during class presentations. I used to feel so embarrassed because of it. Honestly speaking, though, I did sound pretty "unique" (to put it lightly) at the time, and I found that being able to laugh at myself really took a lot of the pressure off.

What's a fruit you can never swallow?
An Adam's apple.

Hair Growth

One sign of puberty is that hair grows in different parts of the body and starts to become coarser. The hormones responsible for hair growth are called androgens. You may start to notice hair grow on your face, around the chin, on the cheeks, and above the lip. Hair also grows on the chest, the armpits, and in the pubic area.

I've had a visible beard and chest hair since sixth grade! I was the first to grow a beard in class. FYI, my beard didn't start off looking like this . . . I remember feeling worried because it was really patchy for years. Eventually, it grew into a full beard. My brother still has empty patches even though he's way past puberty. He says that he worried about it too, but he realized over time that each person's beard just looks different.

Life is like a box of chocolates—you never know which beard you're going to get!

I think it was in tenth grade when there was this one guy in class who didn't have any facial hair at all, and it really got to him. The reason I know this is because I remember this kid telling him his face looked like a baby's butt during one of our soccer games, and that really set him off! First of all, not everyone can grow a beard, and some people prefer not to. Secondly, never compare someone's face to a butt, as much as it may be tempting. Finally, remember that your words matter. I always recall my parents telling me to taste my words before speaking them.

When getting into arguments or disagreeing with your friends, remember that you have control over your actions and not the actions of others. If someone says something that makes you feel uncomfortable:

- Tell them that you don't find it funny and that they need to stop.

- If that doesn't work, talk to an adult about it. Sometimes you need to try more than once to find the right person. It could be a supportive teacher, school counselor, parent, or family member.

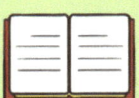 **See "How to Ask for Help" section**

Shaving

When your body is ready, you'll notice hair growth in your pubic area, armpits, chest, and face. The hair does not start to grow on all your body parts all at the same time. It usually (but not always) starts in the pubic area, followed by the armpits. Then you may see hair in your chest area and face. You may be eager to start shaving, but make sure you take the time to learn the right shaving tips to avoid skin irritation and cuts.

I, for one, was really excited to start shaving, and like I mentioned before, I started growing facial hair before any of the other boys in class. Having an older brother made it a lot easier for me cuz he'd been shaving for a couple of years ahead of me, so he was actually the one who taught me how to shave.

When I first started shaving, I was really big on getting a close shave, so I would go back and forth with the razor over the same area. I ended up cutting myself and got skin irritations. I later realized that I only need to go gently over the area I'm shaving once or twice, especially during the early stages of hair growth since the hair isn't as coarse at first.

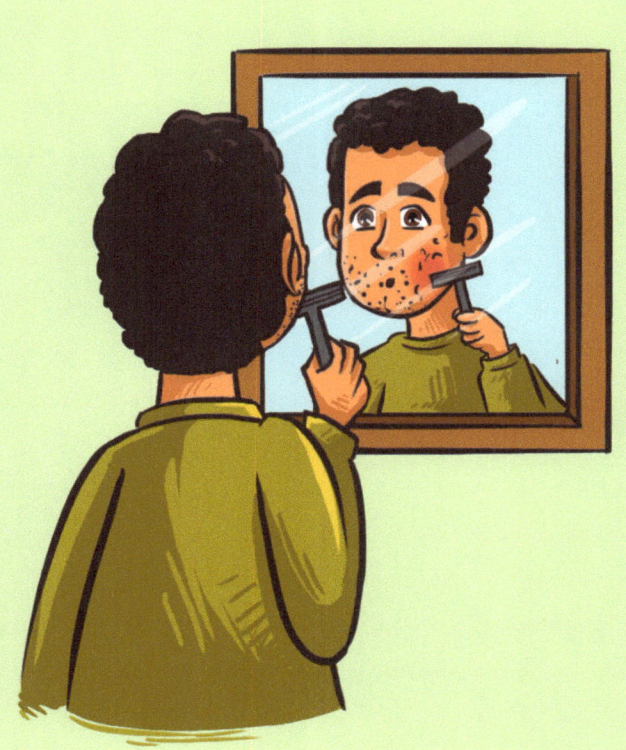

Shaving Tips:

1. Get a parent's or adult's help to purchase a razor.

ELECTRIC RAZOR
(no shaving cream needed and
is less likely to cause cuts)

BLADE RAZOR
(require you to apply shaving cream
and will give you a closer shave)

2. If you are using a blade razor, wet the area you are shaving really well and lather the area with soap or shaving cream. Not applying shaving cream can cause cuts and skin irritations.

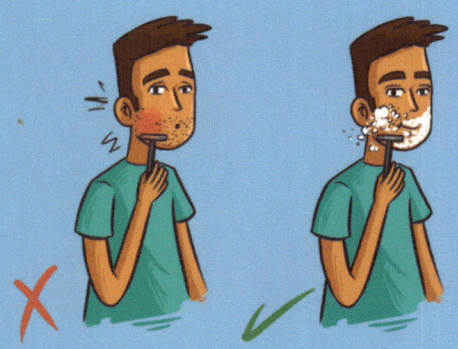

Selecting the right shaving cream or gel may take some time to determine what is best for your skin type.

3. Start by shaving in the direction of the hair growth. Then you can shave in the opposite direction. When shaving, it is best to use short and gentle strokes.

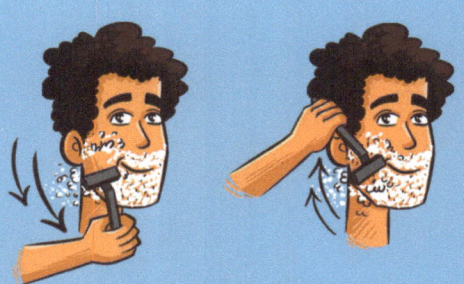

4. Be sure to rinse the razor after each stroke. This prevents nicks and cuts. However, if you do get a small cut, don't worry. Just rinse it well and place a bandage on it if needed.

5. Pat your skin dry with a clean towel and apply moisturizer or aftershave.

Don't underestimate the power of the aftershave and moisturizer! Heads up: applying aftershave can really sting! PRO TIP: to avoid this, get aftershave balm (i.e., alcohol-free aftershave).

 **Never share razors because this can cause skin infections and other skin problems. Also be sure to change your razor after 4 to 5 uses.**

Acne

Man, pimples can really be frustrating! What really got to me were the pimples under my beard. They were itchy and pretty annoying! I don't know if the beard made it worse, but I did go see a dermatologist who prescribed this facial wash, which helped a bit. Eventually, but after what seemed like forever back then, most of the pimples were gone. I still get some pimples under my beard now, and yes, it still itches! My best friend also has adult acne, but it's a lot less now compared to the way it was for him during puberty.

Acne: a skin condition that almost all people experience at different points in life, where red inflamed spots appear on the skin, known as pimples. Many will experience it during puberty, while others get adult acne.

Pimples: small hard inflamed parts on skin that are symptoms of acne

Where does acne come from?

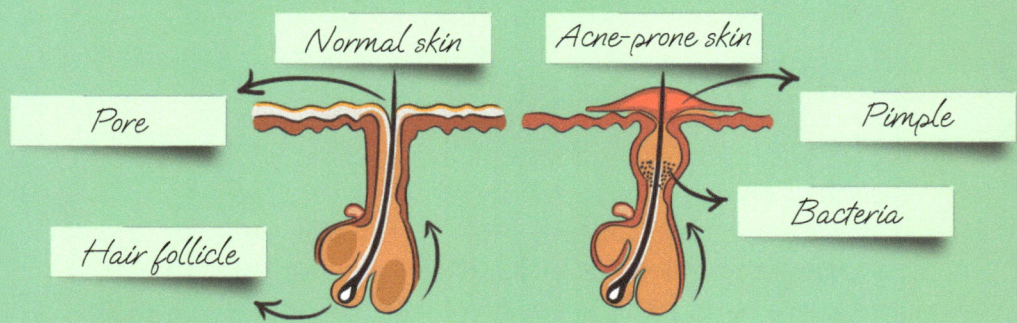

Our skin has small openings called pores that release oils and sweat. The skin also makes sebum, its own natural moisturizer, that keeps our skin soft. Sometimes sebum mixed with bacteria can clog the pores to make a pimple. It's important that we keep our skin clean and try not to touch our face often, so we don't spread bacteria all over it.

It can be tough when you can't hide the pimples and your skin just doesn't look the same. Remember to cut yourself some slack and that most people get pimples at one point in their life or another. Those pimples won't last forever and there is something we can do about it, like applying skin-care products or seeing a dermatologist (a skin doctor). It also helps to express how you're feeling to a friend or adult that you trust.

Some Causes of Acne:

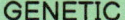

GENETIC

ENVIRONMENTAL

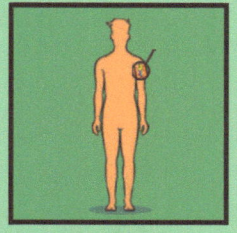

HORMONAL

NUTRITION

Tips for Skin Care:

- Wash your face gently with lukewarm water using mild soap or a cleanser once or twice a day. Avoid scrubbing; it can irritate your skin even more. Pat it dry.

- Avoid popping any pimples because as tempting as it may seem, this can cause scars.

- Make it a habit to change your pillowcases regularly, and frequently wash any facial towels you use to avoid any skin reactions due to bacteria.

- Moisturize your face and body regularly to avoid dry skin.

You can never use too much moisturizer . . . okay, maybe you can, but don't take this lightly. Dry skin can be tough, especially if you struggle with it like me. I never used to really moisturize, but now I actually make it a habit!

Sweat (Body Odor)

Remember those little messenger hormones? One of the ways they manage our body temperature is through sweating!

Have you ever walked into the locker room after gym class? It smells like you stuck your head in a compost bin full of dirty laundry! My contribution was always the feet! I can't even tell you the number of times my mother would yell, "Jamaaaaal, wash your feet!" For real, though, my feet did stink! But hey, my stinky socks came in handy when getting rid of unwanted guests in my room, i.e., my little sister. Sorry Jameela!

So, what causes our sweat to smell?

We have bacteria all over our skin. We also have apocrine sweat glands in our armpits, chest, and pubic area that release fats and proteins. When bacteria feed on the fats and proteins, an unpleasant smell is produced by the bacteria's waste.

It's important that we clean our bodies with water and soap so that we don't smell. There are some areas on our bodies that are more prone to causing unpleasant odors when sweating. Those areas require cleaning and washing more regularly than the rest of the body. We don't just sweat from our armpits, we can also get sweaty in our pubic area.

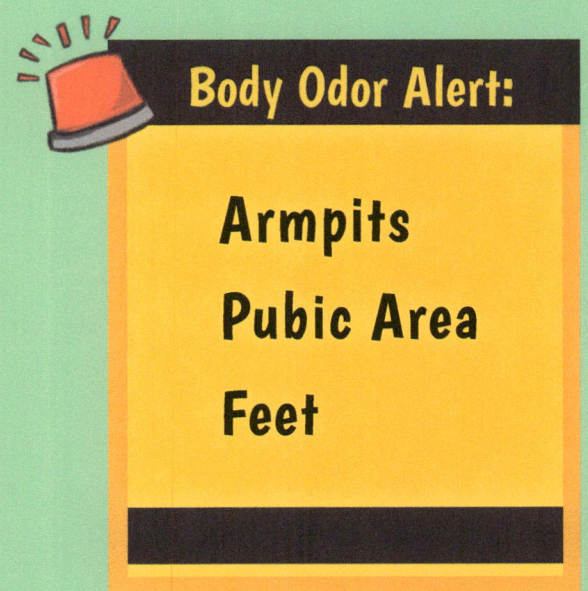

Body Odor Alert:

Armpits

Pubic Area

Feet

Armpits:

Taking a shower and washing your armpit area with soap and water first thing in the morning or after being out in the heat is a good habit to keep you fresh. Make sure you throw your undershirt in the hamper and grab a clean one because wearing the same undershirt can result in an unpleasant smell due to dried-up sweat stains.

Even after showering and changing your undershirt, you might want to use deodorant.

 **ANTIPERSPIRANT**
(reduces the amount we sweat)

 **DEODORANT**
(adds a pleasant smell)

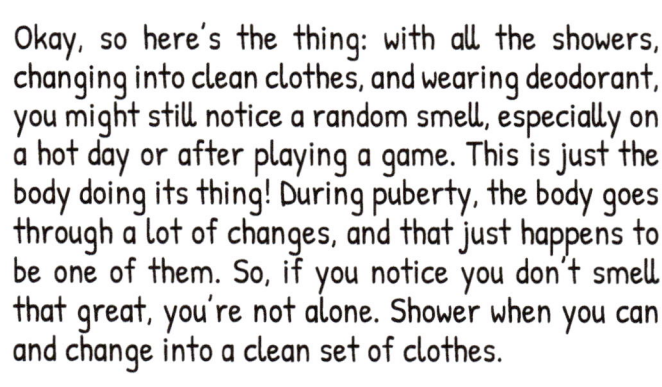

Okay, so here's the thing: with all the showers, changing into clean clothes, and wearing deodorant, you might still notice a random smell, especially on a hot day or after playing a game. This is just the body doing its thing! During puberty, the body goes through a lot of changes, and that just happens to be one of them. So, if you notice you don't smell that great, you're not alone. Shower when you can and change into a clean set of clothes.

 Check out the "In a Pickle" section at the end for body odor

Feet:

As you get older and throughout your years of puberty, you may start to notice that your feet smell, especially when you play sports. Once you get home, wash your feet with soap and water, and don't wear the same pair of socks twice. If you find that your shoes are smelly, you should place them in a cool place to air out and occasionally put baking soda in them to help keep them fresh.

PRO TIP: just stick a tea bag in each shoe or throw in some dryer sheets

"Bruh, that stinks!"

Pubic Area:

To keep your pubic area fresh, it's important to wash and dry this area and make it a habit to change your underwear regularly.

When urine splashes all over the toilet seat it will probably also get on your pants, and it's going to stink. So, make sure you aim for the toilet and if it lands on the seat, make sure you clean up after yourself.

The "P Word"

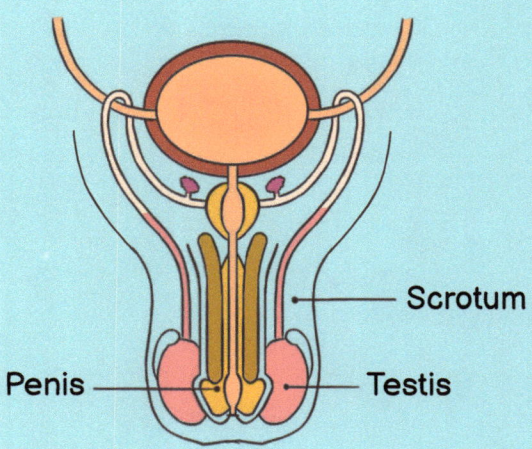

Scrotum

Penis — Testis

Here it is, the section you've all been waiting for. Thinking to yourself, "Man, I wonder what Jamal's gonna say about the penis?" And the answer is not much because I'm guessing you've already been thinking and talking about it way too much. So, I'm just going to keep it simple. They're called PRIVATE PARTS for a reason. No one should ever ask to see or touch your private parts or anyone else's for that matter. When you feel uncertain or uncomfortable with something that is being said or done, speak to an adult you trust.

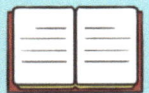

See "How to Ask for Help" section

Privacy does not start at the age of puberty, it starts from when you are a baby. It just looks different as you grow older and become more independent.

P.S. Contrary to popular belief, it's perfectly normal to not want to get changed in front of others.

Consent: when you give your consent, you give your approval for something to happen

Check out the "In a Pickle" at the end for privacy

Let's Talk Facts:

A boy may have adult-size genitals as early as age 13 or as late as 18. First the penis grows in length, then in width.

About a year after your testicles grow bigger, you may have what's known as an "ejaculation" from your penis.

I will also say this: be wary of it. The penis can be a sneaky character, popping into life at the most random times and even in your sleep! A couple of things come to mind here: unexpected erections and wet dreams.

Erection: (your penis getting hard) can be triggered by your thoughts, a movement, or by nothing at all!

Trust me I've been there and thank the lord that baggy clothes were in style back then!

Check out the "In a Pickle" section at the end for unexpected erections

✏️ **Ejaculation:** This happens when muscle movements in your penis cause semen (a sticky fluid mixed with sperm) to squirt out

✏️ **Wet Dream:** When you ejaculate in your sleep

Wet dreams may seem confusing at first, but they are completely normal and are nothing to be embarrassed about.

When we are asleep, the body's breathing, heart rate, and temperature change, which makes the penis more sensitive and more likely to be aroused. Sometimes the ejaculation is caused by a sexual dream, which you may or may not remember.

A penis doesn't need to be big to pee or reproduce. Size only matters as much as you let it.

Around 85 percent of males overestimate what the average penis size actually is.

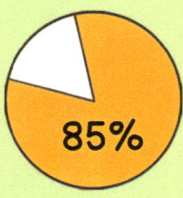

85%

Check "In a Pickle" for what to do after a wet dream

Comparing with Others

Listen, your body is so much more than just your penis. I know it can feel like all your thoughts and actions are controlled by your friend down there, but trust me; life does not revolve around him (as much as he may want you to believe that!). And hey, I know you're probably thinking, "Well that's easy for you to say Jamal, you're old!" And to that I say:

- First of all, 25 is NOT OLD, okay!

- Secondly, if you do consider me old, then you best be respecting your elders!

- Finally, and more seriously, man what I would give to be able to take one moment to try and think a little clearer back then. That's honestly what really matters! Being able to think clearly and healthily manage my thoughts during puberty would've been like having a superpower. Yes, the physicality of puberty does have its moments, but it's the mental game that we really need to be playing.

Expressing Yourself

Speaking of the mental game . . . I told you I was smooth! #whatasegway

Always remember that what you're consuming online and offline will have an impact on your thoughts and feelings.

Nowadays we are bombarded with information, which means there is also a lot of misinformation. Figuring out which is which can be difficult. There are so many messages around us about what it means to be masculine.

Take a look at these statements about masculinity and mental health. Which ones do you think are true?

Answer key on page 48

- [ ] Boys don't cry.
- [ ] It's okay to not have the answer to every question.
- [ ] Don't bother other people with your problems.
- [ ] Don't be a softy.
- [ ] Friends can support each other by sharing their feelings.
- [ ] You are the only one that needs help.
- [ ] Meaningful relationships are built with empathy.
- [ ] Feelings are for girls.
- [ ] It's healthy to express your feelings.
- [ ] Everyone needs help throughout their lives.
- [ ] There are different ways to express yourself.
- [ ] It's okay if I don't know exactly how I am feeling sometimes.

Empathy: the ability to understand and connect with someone else's feelings

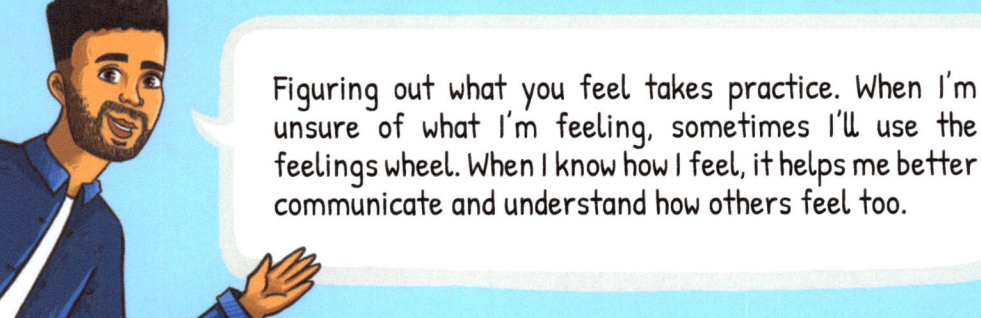

Figuring out what you feel takes practice. When I'm unsure of what I'm feeling, sometimes I'll use the feelings wheel. When I know how I feel, it helps me better communicate and understand how others feel too.

People experience puberty differently. Some may feel a little left out, and others will experience feelings of discomfort. Some people might not experience any discomfort at all. We can feel confused and uninformed. We are all unique and so are our experiences.

Just like physical health, we all have mental health, and it's just as important! Taking care of our mental health includes exercise, nutrition, a sleep routine, healthy relationships, noticing our emotions, speaking kindly to ourselves, and so much more!

I realized how important expressing myself was because of the stomachaches I started getting. Yeah, who knew that not talking about feelings could give you a stomachache?! My doctor said that sometimes physical symptoms can show up when feelings pile up. Something that helps me when I'm getting overwhelmed is to stop and NOTICE.

N – not alone
O – oak tree
T – temporary feelings
I – identify feelings
C – communicate feelings
E – extra practice

N - Not Alone 	I'm not the only one going through this; many others experience the same thing and can relate to my feelings and experiences.
O - Oak Tree 	I'm like an oak tree, with strong roots in the ground and a sturdy trunk. Stop, take a deep breath (breathe in from your nose and fill up your stomach like a balloon, then slowly breathe out from your mouth), stand tall like an oak tree, with your feet firmly planted on the ground. Imagine the roots holding you down.
T - Temporary Feelings 	I know the feeling will pass. It is only temporary. Feelings come and go; they don't last forever.

If you find that applying all the "NOTICE" steps is too much, it's okay; you don't have to do it all. Choose the ones that work best for you depending on how you're feeling at the time.

What come and go and sometimes feel like a roller coaster ride? Our feelings!

I - Identify Feelings 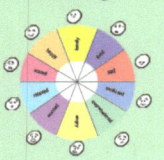	I name the feelings that are showing up for me right now. Sometimes there are more than one at the same time. For example, I could be feeling frustrated, angry, and confused all at the same time.
C - Communicate Feelings 	I communicate my feelings in different ways. I can do this by journaling or talking to a friend or someone I trust. Feelings can also be expressed through art (drawing, poetry, drama, dance, music), and in different communities of faith, they can be expressed through prayer or storytelling.
E - Extra Practice	I am not discouraged if I don't feel better right away. It takes extra practice to learn to be there for myself.

My favorites are O and C. The oak tree helps me calm down, and I communicate my feelings by writing them down or talking to one of my close friends. If there's one takeaway it is that asking for help does not make you weak; if anything, it's a skill that builds your resilience.

 Resilience: the ability to adapt to different circumstances and bounce back from challenging times

How to Ask for Help?

I'm pretty sure you've heard the saying, "There's no such thing as a stupid question." Well, let me tell you, that is completely true! Now how to go about asking the question and speaking your mind, that can feel like a bit of a slippery slope, right? I mean hey, I still struggle with it sometimes! But man have I come a long way. Expressing yourself is honestly just something that takes practice. And remember, just as you may feel you are struggling with it, so are some of your peers. So do your best to be present for them. That may look like being someone they can talk to, checking in on them every once in a while, or maybe just telling them the best and most eye-roll -worthy dad joke you know!

I'm working on a puberty joke . . . but it's not fully developed yet!

If you do feel like there is something really bothering you that you think is better for an adult to hear, then try bringing it up to someone you trust. It could be a family member, teacher, coach, youth worker, or school counselor. Whoever it ends up being, you don't always have to speak to them directly. If you are more comfortable sending a text/email/letter, then by all means do it. What matters is getting it out there.

You know how hard it is to ask for help. So when someone asks for your help or confides in you, treat them and what they tell you with care.

3 Rs

Sleep

If you know me, and know that I haven't gotten enough sleep, avoid me at all costs . . . you have been warned! My parents would open the blinds, pull off the covers, and scream, "JAMAAAAAL! WAKE UP!" None of it worked, even though I had been sleeping for hours. I wasn't ignoring them or being stubborn. I was ASLEEP! I hated getting lectured for not waking up on time just because my brother and sister were up and ready. If that sounds familiar, believe me, you are not alone! It's natural with all the changes your body is going through that you will need to sleep well. The good news is, this doesn't last forever.

Speaking of sleeping well, I found that having a sleep routine really improved my quality of sleep and how I felt the next morning.

1 screens off

2 down time

Sleep hygiene

3 bedtime

Getting enough sleep is very important because it impacts our growth and our overall mood. While we're asleep, our brain is hard at work! Growth hormones are traveling in our bodies, information is being stored and processed, healing is taking place, and harmful substances are released. Sleep also keeps many other hormones balanced. When our hormone levels are irregular, it can impact our moods and how our body feels throughout the day.

Movement

When we move, "feel good" hormones are released, and this can boost our mood and increase our energy levels.

Keep in mind that what we put in our bodies also impacts our mood and how active we can be. I was always told not to worry about what I put in my body and that I'd just grow out of it. FAKE NEWS.

As you notice all the changes your body is going through during puberty, don't forget to appreciate all the amazing things your body is capable of doing! Those "feel good" hormones released with physical activity will not necessarily make you feel good after one basketball game—you have to get in the habit of being active, then you'll see how it can really lift your mood! Some people love to play team sports and others prefer biking, skating, or going for a run. Make sure you're staying active by choosing what works for you and what you enjoy! As long as you are doing what it takes to release those "feel good" hormones!

Guys, trivia, do you know what the most popular sport in the world is? Soccer (or football if you want to be proper) with about 4 billion fans worldwide. Guess what? I'm not one of those 4 billion. It was hard to feel like the odd one out and have to worry about whether I was going to be the last one picked to join someone's team. I felt so many emotions: sadness, frustration, anger, and loneliness. Straight up, being excluded is tough. I found that having supportive people to talk to really helped. Shout out to my older brother and my day-ones.

All this to say, soccer was not for me, but man did I love dodgeball! To this day, I'm in a weekly competitive dodgeball league. Hey! It helps me take out my frustrations—it boosts my mood and keeps me active.

We all have different ways of moving, learning, and experiencing the world. Each of our bodies moves differently, and it's important to explore different variations of movements, sports, or exercises that work best for us. For example, engaging in chair exercises, power chair sports, or going on a walk using an aid.

What's a kind of exercise that isn't really helpful? Running away from your problems!

Girls' Puberty

You know how going through puberty can be confusing? Girls go through it too. They go through different changes than we do because their bodies are different. Some girls will get their period earlier and others later. Sometimes girls are taller or shorter, have more acne, and are at different stages in their breast development. We all know that going through so many changes can be challenging, so in the wise words of my parents, taste your words before you speak them . . . thanks, Mom and Dad.

In a Pickle

1. WET DREAMS

I wake up in the morning to find that I'm a little wet and sticky. I realize I had a wet dream. What do I do?

a)   I throw my sheets and underwear in the hamper to be washed and take a shower.

b)   If there's a small wet area on the bedsheets, I wipe it with wipes or a paper towel, and freshen myself up.

c)   I just ignore it and throw my covers on top. It will dry up anyway.

2. UNEXPECTED ERECTION

While in class I notice my penis erect after a random movement. What do I do about it?

a)   Shift my position and draw my attention elsewhere.

b)   Scratch my calves.

c)   Cover it with a bag, sweater, or other clothes if I'm uncomfortable.

3. BODY ODOR

I've been biking to school and I find that I don't smell that great with the weather being so hot! What do I do?

a)   Spray perfume to try to cover the smell.

b)   Shower and make sure to use deodorant before leaving home.

c)   Use wet paper towels to wipe my underarm area, and have a deodorant and extra shirt packed in my bag on days I bike to school or have gym class.

4. CHANGING IN PUBLIC

One of the boys walks in the gym change room and opens the curtain while I'm still undressed to tell me to hurry up. I feel uncomfortable. What do I do?

a)   Tell him that it is not okay for him to do that, and speak to an adult I trust if it is repeated.

b)   I just keep my feelings to myself and make sure I change quickly.

c)   Tell him that I am not okay with that and to not repeat it. If there is a changing room with a door I can lock, I use that space instead.

5. SWELLING CHEST AREA

I throw on a shirt and I don't feel comfortable with the way it fits at the chest area! What do I do?

a)   Change into a shirt that's baggier or wear a fitted undershirt underneath.

b)   I'm not sure what to do about it yet. So I try to name my feelings using the feelings wheel and practice some NOTICE skills.

c)   I tell myself I need to get over myself and toughen up.

6. FEELING DOWN AND IRRITABLE OR STRONG FEELINGS

One of my family members is going through a difficult time, and it's impacting me as well. I notice that I'm feeling more down or irritable.

a)   I spend more time on my phone and playing video games to distract myself.

b)   I use some of the skills from NOTICE. I also remind myself that reaching out builds resilience and I reach out to someone I trust.

c)   I avoid everyone and stay in my room every time I'm home.

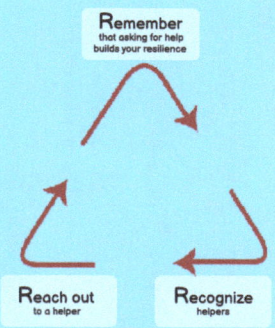

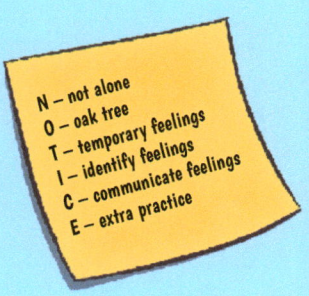

N – not alone
O – oak tree
T – temporary feelings
I – identify feelings
C – communicate feelings
E – extra practice

Keep in mind that these answers are just one of many options to address difficult situations that come up. You may come up with other options that are helpful and just as valid.

IN A PICKLE ANSWER KEY

1. a and b;
2. a and c;
3. b and c;
4. a and c;
5. a and b;
6. b

PAGE 30 ANSWER KEY

1. x
2. ✓
3. x
4. x
5. ✓
6. x
7. ✓
8. x
9. ✓
10. ✓
11. ✓
12. ✓

Glossary

Acne: a skin condition that almost all people experience at different points in life, where red inflamed spots appear on the skin, known as pimples. Many will experience it during puberty, while others get adult acne.

Adam's apple: a small bulge in the throat area that results from the larynx growing and tilting

Adolescent: the time frame in life that starts from puberty until adulthood

Apocrine Sweat Glands: sweat glands that occur at the time of puberty and are found in certain parts of the body such as the armpits, chest, and pubic areas

Consent: when you give your consent, you give your approval for something to happen

Dermatologist: a doctor that diagnoses and treats skin conditions

Ejaculation: when muscle movements in your penis cause semen (a sticky fluid mixed with sperm) to squirt out

Empathy: the ability to understand and connect with someone else's feelings

Erection: (your penis getting hard) can be triggered by your thoughts, a movement, or by nothing at all

Growth hormones: chemicals that deliver messages to different parts of the body to stimulate growth

Hormones: chemicals that deliver messages to different parts of your body. These chemicals start the changes we see in puberty.

Larynx: an organ in your throat where your vocal cords are located, that leads from your throat to your lungs

Penis: the male reproductive organ through which urine and semen pass

Pimples: small hard inflamed parts on skin that are symptoms of acne

Puberty: a stage in your life when your body is going through many changes, both on the inside and outside, to get you ready to be an adult one day

Resilience: the ability to adapt to different circumstances and bounce back from challenging times

Scrotum: a pouch of skin containing the testes

Testes (testicles): an organ that produces sperm

Vocal cords: small muscles in the larynx that vibrate and create sound

Wet Dream: when you ejaculate in your sleep

Meet the Authors

Hoda Elshayeb is a PQ Coach™ (Positive Intelligence®), a certified Life Coach, and a certified Mastery Coach, specializing in TCM (Transformational Coaching Method). She works with clients to identify and overcome self-limiting beliefs, transform negative patterns, and cultivate a more empowered and authentic sense of self. With over 16 years of experience as an educator, mentor, and coach for adults and youth, she has organized and led programs on self-esteem, teamwork, and leadership. She is the founder of *Coach Hoda*, offering one-on-one and group coaching programs that focus on mental fitness leading to greater confidence, improved performance, and deeper connections. She has a passion for personal growth and development, and believes in the power of mental fitness to transform lives. Hoda's known as the full-of-life, spaghetti-loving, bike-is-her-car kinda gal!

Wala'a Farahat is a Registered Psychotherapist, member of the Canadian Association for Play Therapy, and cofounder of Rubiks Counselling Services. Rubiks Counselling Services is an organization shifting how mental health services are provided to diverse populations through accessible and culturally responsive education and therapy. She has extensive experience working with refugees, newcomers, and BIPOC communities, and has worked in various community settings. Wala'a believes in the importance of accessible mental health education and services that allow us to challenge narratives and break cycles as people of color. Her research interests include refugee mental health, trauma, migration, identity, racism, and spirituality. From a young age, Wala'a was known for her huge imagination, bubbly personality, and constant giggles—all things that may have led her to play therapy!

FEATURING BURAIDAH RAZACK

Buraidah Razack is a mental health worker and educator with more than 8 years of experience in youth work and mentorship. He is currently completing his Master of Social Work in the hopes of creating and developing culturally responsive and inclusive mental health resources for members of various faith groups. Buraidah is an avid foodie and a sucker for a good "dad joke" (which may or may not have influenced the contents of this book).

Our Mission

To provide age-appropriate, representative, diverse resources for tweens and teens addressing themes of self-development, self-esteem, and identity.

Contact Us

Feel free to get in touch to schedule a consultation, book reading, workshop, or custom package to meet your needs!

Email iykyk.edu@gmail.com
or visit www.iykykteens.com.

IF YOU KNOW, YOU KNOW!

Books for Preteens and Teens

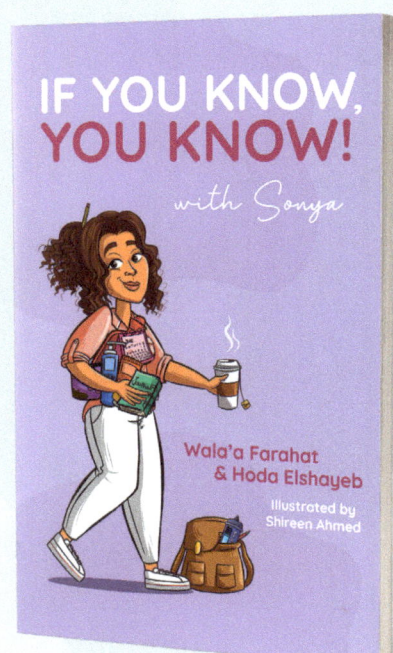

Purchase at
www.iykykteens.com

www.ingramcontent.com/pod-product-compliance
Lightning Source LLC
Chambersburg PA
CBHW040905120626
46551CB00006B/651